Building a State in Apache Land

Charles D. Poston

Contents

I How the Territory Was Acquired 7
II Early Mining and Filibustering 17
III War-Time in Arizona 32
IV Arizona a Territory at Last 42

BUILDING A STATE IN APACHE LAND

BY

Charles D. Poston

I
How the Territory Was Acquired

In San Francisco in the early fifties, there was a house on the northeast corner of Stockton and Washington, of considerable architectural pretensions for the period, which was called the "Government Boarding House."

The cause of this appellation was that the California senators and their families, a member of Congress and his wife, the United States marshal, and several lesser dignitaries of the Federal Government, resided there. In those early days private mansions were few; so the boarding-house formed the only home of the Argonauts.

After the ladies retired at night, the gentlemen usually assembled in the spacious parlor, opened a bottle of Sazerac, and discussed politics.

It was known to the senators that the American minister in Mexico had been instructed to negotiate a new treaty with Mexico for the acquisition of additional territory; not that there was a pressing necessity for more land, but for reasons which will be briefly stated:

1st. By the treaty of 1848, usually called Guadaloupe Hidalgo,[A] the government of the United States had undertaken to protect the Mexicans from the incursions of Indians within the United States boundary, and as this proved to be an impractical undertaking, the damages on account of failure began to assume alarming proportions, and the government of the United States was naturally anxious to be released from the obligation.

2. The Democratic party was in the plenitude of power, and the Southern States were dominant in the Administration. It had been the dream of this element for many years to construct a railroad from the Mississippi River to the Pacific

Ocean, and the additional territory was required for "a pass". It was not known at that early day that railroads could be constructed across the Rocky Mountains at a higher latitude, and it was feared that snow and ice might interfere with traffic in the extremes of winter.

The State of Texas had already given encouragement to the construction of such a railroad, by a liberal grant of land reaching as far west as the Rio Grande, and it devolved upon the United States to provide the means of getting on to the Pacific Ocean. The intervening country belonged at that time to Mexico, and for the purpose of acquiring this land the treaty was authorized.

The condition of affairs in Mexico was favorable to a negotiation. Santa Ana had usurped the powers of the government, and was absolute dictator under the name of President. There was no Mexican Congress, and none had been convened since they were herded together at the conclusion of the Mexican War under protection of American troops.

The condition of affairs in the United States was also extremely favorable. The treasury was overflowing with California gold, under the tariff of 1846 business was prosperous, the public debt small, and the future unclouded. The American Minister to Mexico (General Gadsden of South Carolina) was authorized to make several propositions:--

1st. Fifty Millions for a boundary line from the mouth of the Rio Grande west to the Pacific Ocean.

2nd. Twenty millions for a boundary line due east from the mouth of the Yaqui River in the Gulf of Mexico to the Rio Grande. This was to include the peninsula of Lower California.

3rd. Ten millions for a boundary line to include the "railroad pass."

A treaty was finally concluded for the smaller boundary, including the "railroad pass," comprising the land between the Rio Grande and the Colorado Rivers south of the Gila River, with the boundary line between the United States and Mexico about the shape of a dog's hind leg. The price paid for the new territory, which was temporarily called the "Gadsden Purchase," was ten million dollars.

A check for seven million was given by Mr. Guthrie, Secretary of the Treasury, on the sub-treasury in New York, to the agent of Santa Ana; but not a dollar of it ever reached the Mexican treasury, as Santa Ana fled with the spoil. The remaining three millions were retained to pay the "lobby" and confirm the treaty. The treaty was signed in Mexico on the 23d day of December, 1853.

Pending the negotiation of the treaty between the high contracting parties, in the City of Mexico, the discussion of the subject grew interesting at the Government Boarding-House in San Francisco, and a new California was hoped for on the southern boundary. Old Spanish history was ransacked for information from the voyages of Cortez in the Gulf of California to the latest dates, and maps of the country were in great demand.

In the mean time an agent of the Iturbide family had arrived in San Francisco with a "Mexican Grant." After the execution of the Emperor Iturbide, the Congress of the Mexican Republic voted an indemnity to the family of one million dollars; but on account of successive revolutions this sum was never at the disposition of the Mexican treasury, and in liquidation the Mexican government made the family a grant of land in California, north of the Bay of San Francisco, but before the land could be located, the Americans had "acquired" the country, and it was lost. The heirs then made application to the Mexican government for another grant of land in lieu of the California concession, and were granted seven hundred leagues of land, to be located in Sonora, Sinaloa and Lower California, in such parcels as they might select.

Seven hundred leagues, or 3,000,800 acres, is a large tract of land in a single body, and the attorney of the heirs considered it more convenient to locate the land in small tracts of a league or two at a place. The government of Mexico conceded whatever was required, and the grant was made in all due form of Mexican law.

In the discussion at the Government Boarding House in San Francisco it was urged: That the Gulf of California was the Mediterranean of the Pacific, and its waters full of pearls. That the Peninsula of Lower California was copper-bound, interspersed with gold and minerals, illustrated with old Spanish Missions, and fanned by the gentlest breezes from the South Pacific. That the State of Sonora was one of the richest of Mexico in silver, copper, gold, coal and other materials, with highly productive agricultural valleys in the temperate zone. That the country north of Sonora, called in the Spanish history "Arizunea" (rocky country) was full of minerals, with fertile valleys washed by numerous rivers, and covered by forests primeval. That the climate was all that could be desired, from the level of the Gulf of California, to an altitude of 15,000 feet in the mountains of the north. That the Southern Pacific Railroad would soon be built through the new country, and that a new State would be made as a connecting link between Texas and California, with the usual quota of governors, senators, and public officials.

It was urged that the Iturbide Grant could be located so as to secure the best sites for towns and cities in the new State, and the rest distributed to settlers as an inducement for rapid colonization. The enthusiasm increased with the glamour of Spanish history and the generous flow of Sazerac.

It must be admitted that an alluring prospect was opened for a young man idling away his life over a custom house desk at three hundred dollars a month; and in the enthusiasm of youth I undertook to make an exploration of the new territory and to locate the Iturbide Grant. Who could have foreseen that the attempted location of the Iturbide Grant would upset the Mexican Republic and set up an empire in Mexico under French protection?

The first thing was to organize a "syndicate" in San Francisco, to furnish funds for expenses and for the location of the Iturbide Grant. This was easily accomplished through some enthusiastic French bankers.

The ex-member of Congress was dispatched to the City of Mexico to secure the approbation of the Mexican government, and I embarked at San Francisco for Guaymas with a rather tough cargo of humanity. They were not so bad as reckless; not ungovernable, but independent.

The records of the United States consulate in Guaymas, if they are preserved, show our registration as American citizens, fourteenth day of January, 1854. The Mexican officials were polite, but not cordial. They said Santa Ana had no right to sell the territory, as he was an usurper and possessed no authority from the Mexican people. As international tribunals had not then been established to determine these nice points of international ethics, we did not stop to argue the question, but pushed on to the newly acquired territory.

We were very much disappointed at its meagerness, and especially that the boundary did not include a port in the Gulf of California. A larger territory could have been secured as easily, but the American Minister had only one idea, and that was to secure "a pass" for a Southern Pacific Railroad from the Mississippi River to the Pacific Ocean. The pass desired was the Guadaloupe Canon, used as a wagon road by General Cook in his march from New Mexico to California in 1846, and strange to say, not subsequently occupied as a railroad pass.

The country south of the new boundary line is not of much consequence to us: it belongs to Mexico.

The country north of the Mexican boundary is the most marvelous in the United States. After many years of arduous investigation and comparison with all the other countries of the world, it is still nearly as great an enigma as when first explored in 1854. The valleys are as fair as the sun ever shone upon, with soil as productive as the valley of the Nile. The rigors of winter never disturb agricultural pursuits in the open. In fact, in the southern portion of the territory there is no winter.

The valleys of Arizona are not surpassed for fertility and beauty by any that I have seen, and that includes the whole world; but still they are not occupied. Spanish and Mexican grants have hung over the country like a cloud, and settlers could not be certain of a clear title. Moreover, the Apaches have been a continual source of dread and danger. This state of affairs is, however, now passing away.

There were evidences of a recent Mexican occupation, with the ruins of towns, missions, presidios, haciendas, and ranches. There were evidences of former Spanish civilization, with extensive workings in mines. There were evidences of a still more remote and mysterious civilization by an aboriginal race, of which we know nothing, and can learn but little by the vestiges they have left upon earth.

They constructed houses, lived in communities, congregated in cities, built fortresses, and cultivated the soil by irrigation. No evidence has been found that they used any domestic animals, no relic of wheeled vehicles, neither iron, steel, nor copper implements; and yet they built houses more than five stories high, and cut joists with stone axes.

How they transported timbers for houses is not known. The engineering for their irrigating canals was as perfect as that practiced on the Euphrates, the Ganges, or the Nile. The ruins of the great houses (casas grandes) are precisely with the cardinal points.

Near Florence, on the Gila, is beyond all doubt the oldest and most unique edifice in the United States. Just when and how it was built baffles human curiosity. Whether it was erected for a temple, a palace, or a town hall, cannot be ascertained. The settlement or city surrounding the ruin must have occupied a radius of quite ten miles, judging from the ruins and pieces of broken pottery within that space. An irrigating canal formerly ran from the Gila River to the city or settlement, for domestic uses and for irrigation.

The Pima Indians have lived in their villages on the Gila River time immemorial, at least they have no tradition of the time of their coming. Their tribal organization has many features worthy imitation by more civilized people. The government rests with a hereditary chief and a council of sages. The rights of property are protected, as far as they have any individual property, which is small, as they are in fact communists. The water from the Gila River to irrigate their lands is obtained by canals constructed by the common labor of the tribe.

In my intercourse with these Indians for many years they frequently asked questions which would puzzle, the most profound philosopher to answer. For instance, they inquired, "Who made the world and everything therein?"

I replied, "God."

"Where does he live?"

"In the sky."

"What does he sit on?"

In their domestic relations they have a system thousands of years older than the Edmunds Act, which works to suit them, and fills the requirements of satisfied nationalities. The old men said the marriage system had given them more trouble than anything else, and they finally abandoned all laws to the laws of nature. The young people were allowed to mate by natural selection, and if they were not satisfied they could "swap."

In after years, when I was Superintendent of Indian Affairs, I selected a stalwart Pima named Luis, who was proud of his acquirements in the English language, and gave him a uniform, sword, and epaulettes about the size of a saucer, to stand guard in front of my quarters.

One day I came out and found Luis walking with an ununiformed Pima, with their arms around each other's waists, according to their custom. I inquired, "Luis, who is that?"

"That is my brother-in-law."

"Did you marry his sister?"

"No."

"Did he marry your sister?"

"No."

"Then how is he your brother-in-law?"

"We swapped wives."

Among the Pimas there is no incentive to avarice, and the accumulation of large personal fortunes. When a Pima dies, most of his personal property, that is, house and household belongings, which he had used during life, is committed to the flames as a sanitary measure, and whatever he may have left of personal property is divided among the tribe.

The dead are buried in the ground in silence, and you can never get the Pimas to pronounce the name of a dead man. The Pimas have many customs resembling the Jews, especially the periodical seclusion of women.

The Apaches have robbed them time immemorial, and they in turn make frequent campaigns against the Apaches. When they return from such a campaign, if they have shed blood they paint their faces black, and seclude themselves from the women. If they have not shed blood they paint their faces white, and enter the joys of matrimony.

The Pima handiwork in earthenware, horsehair, bridle reins, ropes, and domestic utensils, is remarkably ingenious. They formerly cultivated cotton and manufactured cotton cloth of a very strong quality. The men understood spinning and weaving, and passed the winter in this industrial pursuit.

Their subsistence is wheat, corn, melons, pumpkins, vegetables, and the wild fruits. They have herds of cattle, plenty of horses, and great quantities of poultry.

The Americans are indebted to the Pima Indians for provisions furnished the California emigration, and for supplies for the early overland stages, besides their faithful and unwavering friendship.

The habitations of these prehistoric people form the most unique of all the anomalous dwellings of Arizona, and a more minute investigation than has hitherto been made will show the earliest habitations of man. There are similar edifices in Egypt and India, but they are mostly temples. These Arizona cliff dwellings are the only edifices of the kind that are known to have been inhabited by mankind. They exist mostly in the mountains in the northern portion of Arizona. A more ancient race, still, lived in the excavations on the sides of the mountains, prepared, no doubt, as a refuge against enemies.

At the time of our first exploration (1854) there was virtually no civilized population in the recently acquired territory. The old pueblo of Tucson contained probably three hundred Mexicans, Indians, and half breeds. The Pima Indians on the Gila River numbered from seven to ten thousand, and were the only producing population. We could not explore the country north of the Gila River, because of the Apaches, who then numbered fully twenty thousand. For three hundred years they have killed Spaniards, Mexicans, and Americans, which makes about the longest continuous war on record.

It was impossible to remain with a considerable number of men in a country destitute of sustenance; so we followed the Gila River down to its junction with the Colorado, and camped on the bank opposite Fort Yuma, glad to be again in sight of the American flag. The commanding officer, Major--afterwards General--Heintzelman, issued the regulation allowance of emigrant rations, which were very grateful to men who had been living for some time without what are usually called the necessaries of life. Fort Yuma was established in 1851, to suppress the Indians on the Colorado, and to protect emigrants at the crossing.

It was apparent that the junction of the Gila and Colorado must be the seaport of the new territory.

The Colorado was supposed to be navigable nearly seven hundred miles, and steamboats were already at Yuma transporting supplies for the post. By the treaty with Mexico of 1848 the boundary line was established from the mouth of the Rio Grande northwardly to the headwaters of the Gila River, thence along the channel of the Gila River to its confluence with the Colorado. The treaty then says: "From a point at the confluence of the Gila and Colorado rivers, westerly to a point on the Pacific Ocean six miles south of the southernmost point of the Bay of San Diego."

As the geography of the country was not well understood at the time, it was not presumably known to the makers of the treaty that the boundary line would include both banks of the Colorado River in the American boundary, but it does. By a curious turn in the Colorado River, after passing through the gorge between Fort Yuma and the opposite bank, the boundary line of the United States includes both banks of the River to the crossing at Pilot Knob, nearly nine miles. When the State of California was organized in 1850, the constitution adopted the boundary line of the State, and consequently assumed jurisdiction over the slip of land on the bank of the Colorado opposite Fort Yuma. When Fort Yuma was established, the commanding officer established a military reservation, including both banks of the Colorado River at its junction with the Gila.

The boundary line between Mexico and the United States, under the treaty of 1848, was run in 1850, and monuments erected on the southern bank of the Colorado, to indicate the possession of the United States.

While we were encamped on the banks of the Colorado River, in the hot month of July, 1854, we concluded to locate a town-site on the slip of land opposite Fort Yuma, and as we were well provided with treaties, maps, surveying instruments, and stationery, there was not much difficulty in making the location. The actual survey showed 936 acres within the slip, and this was quite large enough for a "town-site." A town-site is generally the first evidence of American civilization.

After locating the town-site at Yuma there was nothing to do but to cross the desert from the Colorado River to San Diego. We made the journey on mules, with extraordinary discomfort. At San Diego we were as much rejoiced as the followers of Xenophon to see the sea.

The town-site was duly registered in San Diego, which could not have been done if both banks of the Colorado just below its junction with the Gila had not been recognized as being within the jurisdiction of the State of California. The county of San Diego collected taxes there for many years. After the organization of the Territory of Arizona in 1863, Arizona assumed jurisdiction over the slip, and built a prison there. Congress subsequently made a grant of land included in the slip to the "Village of Yuma," so that it is a mere question of jurisdiction, not involving the validity of any titles. The question of jurisdiction still remains unsettled, as it requires both an Act of Congress and Act of the State Legislature to change the boundaries of a sovereign State.

The town-site of Yuma has grown slowly, but there will be a town there as long as the two rivers flow. The Southern Pacific Railroad was completed years ago, and forms the great artery of commerce. Immigration enterprises of great magnitude have been undertaken with the waters of the Colorado River. The river washes fully three hundred thousand square miles, and furnishes a water power in the cataracts of the Grand Canon only second to Niagara.

"At Yuma, on the Colorado River, the only attempt at irrigation so far made is by pumping works, which raise the water from the river and convey it in pipes to the lands to be watered. While thus far only a limited area is watered by this method, the results are satisfactory, and the expense no greater than in many of the pipe systems of California.

"But for the magnitude, scope, and the boldness of its purpose, the project to irrigate the great Colorado Desert is without a parallel in the arid West, if in the world.

"This undertaking contemplates the construction of gravity canals from a point in the Colorado River, several miles above Yuma, and the conducting of the waters of this river over an arid waste, that, while forbidding in appearance, is known to be capable of great fertility. One interesting feature of this plan to reclaim the desert is found in the character of the water to be utilized. Analysis shows that the water of the Colorado River carries a larger percentage of sedimentary deposit than any other river in the world, not excepting the Nile. The same is true, in a relative degree, of all the other rivers in Arizona. By constant use of these waters the soil not only receives the reviving benefits of irrigation, but at the same time a very considerable amount of fertilizing material.

"The beneficial results thus made possible have already been practically demonstrated, and what may be achieved by the proposed reclamation of a vast area, with peculiar advantages of climate and environment, is one of the most significant suggestions conceivable in connection with the new era of irrigation.

"The storage of water by reservoirs for irrigation purposes has thus far been one of the untried problems in Arizona. But the possibilities in this section are equal to any section of the arid West, and because of the stability and certainty of this method, it is only a question of time when it will be carried into practical force."[B]

In the progress of civilization, Fort Yuma has given way to an Indian school, where the dusky denizens of the Colorado are progressing in learning.

After concluding our business in San Diego, we took the steamer for San Francisco, and laid the result of the reconnaissance (which was not much) before the "Syndicate." We had an audience with the commanding officer of the Pacific, and procured a recommendation to the Secretary of War for an exploration of the Colorado River. This was subsequently accomplished with beneficial results,--at least for information. In San Francisco it was decided that I should proceed to Washington, for the purpose of soliciting assistance of the Federal Government in opening the new Territory for settlement, and the voyage was made *via* Panama.

* * * * *

NOTES:

[NOTE A: It has been a mystery which I have been asked to explain a thousand times, why the Gadsden Treaty was made with such a boundary line. The true inwardness of the treaty is attempted to be explained. The boundary line at Yuma, on the Colorado, at the junction of the Gila, is now submitted to the U.S. Supreme Court. See Attorney General Hart.--C.D.P.]

[NOTE B: Quoted from a recent article of mine in a local paper. Such quotations will occur in this series without further credit.--C.D.P.]

II
Early Mining and Filibustering

In 1855, When I arrived in Washington as an amateur delegate from the new Territory, the "Gadsden Purchase" did not attract much attention. They had something else to do. President Pierce, the most affable of Presidents, was very polite, and asked many questions about the new acquisition. The Secretary of War, Jefferson Davis, promised to order an exploration of the Colorado River as soon as he could get an appropriation, and to send troops to the new Territory as soon as they could be spared.

During the winter General Heintzelman came to Washington, and as the town was crowded, and he could not find suitable accommodations, I had an extra bed put in my room at the National, and we messed together. It was an advantage to have an officer of the Army who had been in command at Yuma to give information about the country, and the association thus formed lasted through life.

There was not much to be done in Washington, so I went over to New York, the seat of "The Texas Pacific Railroad Company." This company had been organized under a munificent land grant from the State of Texas. The capital stock was a hundred million dollars. The scheme was to build a railroad from the Mississippi River to the Pacific Ocean on the proceeds of land grants and bonds, and make the hundred millions of dollars stock as profit, less one tenth of one per cent to be paid in for expenses and promotion money. The President of this company was Robert J. Walker, Secretary of the Treasury under President Polk; Vice-President, Thomas Butler King, of Georgia, late Collector of the Port in San Francisco, my recent superior; Secretary, Samuel Jaudon, late Cashier of the United States Bank. Mr. Walker, the President of the Company, received me at dinner at his mansion on Fifth Avenue, and my acquaintance with Thomas Butler King was renewed over sparkling vintages.

This company had parcelled the world out among its officers. Robert J. Walker was to have the financial field of Europe. Samuel Jaudon, the secretary, was to display his financial ability in New York and the Atlantic cities. Edgar Conkling, of Cincinnati, was agent for the Mississippi Valley. Thomas Butler King was allotted the State of Texas, and I, being the junior, was to have the country between the Rio Grande and the Colorado.

I told them all I knew about the Territory,--and a great deal more,--and enlarged upon the advantages that would accrue to the railroad company by an exploration of the new Territory and a development of its mineral resources. They inquired how much it would cost to make the exploration. I replied that I would start with a hundred thousand dollars if there was a million behind it.

A company was organized with a capital of two million dollars, and shares sold at an average of fifty dollars. General Heintzelman was appointed president, and I was appointed "manager and commandant." The office was located in Cincinnati, for the convenience of General Heintzelman, who was stationed at Newport Barracks, Ky. William Wrightson was appointed secretary.

As soon as the necessary arrangements were made I started west on this arduous undertaking. The arms and equipments had been shipped to San Antonio, Texas, and I proceeded there to complete the outfit.

San Antonio was the best outfitting place in the Southwest at that time. Wagons, ambulances, mules, horses, and provisions were abundant, and men could be found in Texas willing to go anywhere.

At San Antonio I met the famous George Wilkins Kendall, who advised me to go to New Bramfels, where I could find some educated German miners, and as he was going to Austin I accompanied him as far as New Bramfels, and received the benefit of his introduction. There were plenty of educated German miners about New Bramfels, working on farms and selling lager beer, and they enlisted joyfully. The rest of the company was made up of frontiersmen (buckskin boys), who were not afraid of the devil.

We pulled out of San Antonio, Texas, on the first day of May, 1856, and took the road to El Paso, or Paso del Norte, on the Rio Grande, 762 miles by the itinerary. The plains of Texas were covered with verdure and flowers, and the mocking birds made the night march a serenade.

I carried recommendations from the War Department to the military officers of the frontiers for assistance, if necessary. The first military post on the road was Fort Clark (El Moro), and a beautiful location. The post was at that time under the command of the famous John Bankhead Magruder, whom I had known in California.

Magruder had recently returned from Europe, bringing two French cooks; and as he was a notorious bon vivant, it was not disagreeable to accept an invitation to dinner.

After breakfast next morning I went to take my leave of the officers, but Magruder said:--

"Sir, you cannot go. Consider yourself under arrest."

I replied, "General, I am not aware of having violated any of the regulations of the Army."

"No, sir, but you are violating the rules of hospitality. You shall stay here three days. Send your train on to the Pecos, and I will send an escort with you to overtake it."

So I remained at Fort Clark three days in duress, and never had a prisoner of war more hospitable entertainment. Texas overflows with abundant provisions, if they only had French cooks.

After a toilsome and dangerous march through Lipans and Commanches we arrived on the upper Rio Grande, at El Paso, in time to spend the Fourth of July. El

Paso at this time was enjoying an era of commercial prosperity. The Mexican trade was good. Silver flowed in in a stream.

After recruiting at El Paso we moved up to the crossing of the Rio Grande at Fort Thorn, and prepared to plunge into Apache land. Camping the command on the green-fringed Mimbres I took five men, and with Doctor Steck and his interpreter made a visit to the Apaches in their stronghold at Santa Rita del Cobre.

There was an old triangular-shaped fort built by the Spaniards which afforded shelter. There were about three hundred Apaches in camp,--physically, fine looking fellows who seemed as happy as the day was long. The agent distributed two wagon loads of corn, from which they made "tiz-win," an intoxicating drink.

Their principal business, if they have any, is stealing stock in Mexico and selling it on the Rio Grande. The mule trade was lively. They proved themselves expert marksmen; but I noticed always cut the bullets out of the trees, as they are economists in ammunition if nothing else.

Deer and turkeys were plentiful, and we feasted for several days in the old triangular fort and under the trees. Doctor Steck told the Apaches that I was "a mighty big man," and they must not steal any of my stock nor kill any of my men.

The chiefs said they wanted to be friends with the Americans, and would not molest us if we did not interfere with their "trade with Mexico."

On this basis we made a treaty and the Apaches kept it.

I had a lot of tin-types taken in New York, which I distributed freely among the chiefs, so they might know me if we should meet again. Many years afterwards an Apache girl told me they could have killed me often from ambush, but they remembered the treaty and would not do it. I have generally found the Indians willing to keep faith with the whites, if the whites will keep faith with them.

After leaving the camp at the Mimbres, we crossed the Chiricahua Mountains, and camped for noon on a little stream called the San Simon, which empties into the Gila River. We had scarcely unlimbered when the rear guard called out, "Apaches!" and about a hundred came thundering down the western slope of the mountain, well mounted and well armed. Their horsemanship was admirable, their horses in good condition, and many of them caparisoned with silver-mounted saddles and bridles, the spoil of Mexican foray.

A rope was quickly stretched across the road, the ammunition boxes got out, and everything prepared for a fight. The chief was a fine-looking man named Alessandro, and as a fight was the last thing we desired, a parley was called when they reached the rope.

When asked what they wished, they said they wanted to come into camp and trade; that they had captives, mules, mescal, and so on. We told them we were not traders, and had nothing to sell. They were rather insolent at this, and made some demonstrations against the rope. I told the interpreter to say that I would shoot the first man that crossed the rope, and they retired for consultations. Finally they thought better of it, or did not like the looks of our rifles and pistols, and struck off for their homes in the north.

I had a stalwart native of Bohemia in the company who was considered very brave; but when the attack was imminent he was a little slow in coming forward, and I cried out somewhat angrily, "Anton, why don't you come out?"

He replied, "Wait till I light my pipe." And that Dutchman stalked out with a rifle in his hand, two pistols on his sides, and a great German pipe in his mouth.

The Apaches did not trouble us any more, and after crossing high mountains and wide valleys we arrived on the Santa Cruz River, and camped at the old Mission Church of San Xavier del Bac.

Three leagues north of the Mission Church of San Xavier del Bac (Bac means water) is located the ancient and honorable pueblo of Tucson. This is the most ancient pueblo in Arizona, and is first mentioned in Spanish history in the narrative of Castaneda, in 1540. The Spanish expedition of Coronado in search of gold stopped here awhile, and washed some gold from the sands of the Canon del Oro on sheep skins. It is well known that that expedition drove sheep. The Spaniards, from this experience, remembering the island of Colchis, named the place Tucson,--Jason in Spanish. The "ancient and honorable pueblo" has borne this name ever since, without profound knowledge of its origin.

The patron saint of Tucson is San Augustine, and as it was now the last of August the fiesta in honor of her patron saint was being celebrated.

As we had a long march and a dry time, the animals were sent out to graze in charge of the Papago Indians living around the Missions; two weeks' furlough was given the men to attend the fiesta, confess their sins, and get acquainted with the Mexican senoritas, who flocked there in great numbers from the adjoining State of

Sonora.

Music and revelry were continued day and night, with very few interruptions by violence. The only disorder that I observed was caused by a quarrel among some Americans, and the use of the infernal revolver. There were not more than a dozen Americans in the pueblo of Tucson when we arrived, and they were not Methodist preachers. The town has grown with the country, and now contains a population of nearly ten thousand people, of many shades of color and many nationalities.

The first question to be settled was the location of a headquarters for the company. We had come a long way, at considerable risk and expense, and fortunately without disaster. We were now encamped in view of the scene of our future operations, and the exploration and settlement of a territory of considerably over a hundred thousand square miles was before us, and the destiny of a new State was in embryo. It would not be prudent to expose the lives of the men and valuable property we had hauled so far to the cupidity of the natives; and therefore a safe place for storage and for defense was the first necessity in selecting a headquarters. We had some hundred and fifty horses and mules, wagons, ambulances, arms, provisions, merchandise, mining, material,--and moreover, what we considered of inestimable value, the future,--in our keeping, and a proper location was a grave consideration.

The Spaniards had located a presidio at the base of the Santa Rita Mountains on the Santa Cruz River, a stream as large and as beautiful as the Arno, flowing from the southeast, and watering opulent valleys which had been formerly occupied and cultivated. The presidio was called Tu-bac (the water). The Mexican troops had just evacuated the presidio of Tubac, leaving the quarters in a fair state of preservation, minus the doors and windows, which they hauled away.

The presidio of Tubac was about ten leagues south of the mission church of San Xavier del Bac, on the Santa Cruz River, on the high road (camino real) to Sonora and Mexico; consequently we struck camp at the Mission San Xavier del Bac, and pulled out for the presidio of Tubac to establish our headquarters and future home.

There was not a soul in the old presidio. It was like entering the ruins of Pompeii. Nevertheless we set to work, cleaned out the quarters, repaired the corrals, and prepared to make ourselves as comfortable as possible.

The first necessity in a new settlement is lumber, and we dispatched men to the adjacent mountains of Santa Rita to cut pine with whip-saws, and soon had lumber for doors, windows, tables, chairs, bedsteads, and the primitive furniture necessary for housekeeping. The quarters could accommodate about three hundred men, and the corrals were ample for the animals. The old quartel made a good storehouse, and the tower on the north, of which three stories remained, was utilized as a lookout. The beautiful Santa Cruz washed the eastern side of the presidio, and fuel and grass were abundant in the valley and on the mountain sides. It was not more than a hundred leagues to Guaymas, the seaport of the Gulf of California, where European merchandise could be obtained. There were no frontier custom houses at that time to vex and hinder commerce.

In the autumn of 1856 we had made the headquarters for the company at Tubac comfortable, laid in a store of provisions for the winter, and were ready to begin the exploration of the country for mines. When you look at the Santa Rita Mountains from Tubac, it seems a formidable undertaking to tunnel and honeycomb them for mines. Nevertheless, we began to attack with stout hearts and strong arms, full of hope and enthusiasm. The mines in the Santa Rita Mountains had been previously worked by the Spaniards and Mexicans, as was evident by the ruins of arrastres and smelters. Gold could be washed on the mountain sides, and silver veins could be traced by the discolored grass.

As soon as it was known in Mexico that an American company had arrived in Tubac, Mexicans from Sonora and the adjacent States came in great numbers to work, and skillful miners could be employed at from fifteen to twenty-five dollars a month and rations. Sonora furnished flour, beef, beans, sugar, barley, corn, and vegetables, at moderate prices.

A few straggling Americans came along now and then on pretense of seeking employment. When questioned on that delicate subject, they said they would work for $10 a day and board; that they got that in California, and would never work for less. After staying a few days at the company's expense they would reluctantly move on, showing their gratitude for hospitality by spreading the rumor that "the managers at Tubac employed foreigners and greasers, and would not give a white man a chance." They were generally worthless, dissipated, dangerous, low white trash.

Many Mexicans that had been formerly soldiers at the presidio of Tubac had little holdings of land in the valley, and returned to cultivate their farms, in many cases accompanied by their families.

By Christmas, 1856, an informal census showed the presence of fully a thousand souls (such as they were) in the valley of the Santa Cruz in the vicinity of Tubac. We had no law but love, and no occupation but labor. No government, no taxes, no public debt, no politics. It was a community in a perfect state of nature. As "syndic" under New Mexico, I opened a book of records, performed the marriage ceremony, baptized children, and granted divorces.

Sonora has always been famous for the beauty and gracefulness of its senoritas. The civil wars in Mexico, and the exodus of the male population from Northern Mexico to California, had disturbed the equilibrium of population, till in some pueblos the disproportion was as great as a dozen females to one male; and in the genial climate of Sonora this anomalous condition of society was unendurable. Consequently the senoritas and grass widows sought the American camp on the Santa Cruz River. When they could get transportation in wagons hauling provisions they came in state,--others came on the hurricane deck of burros, and many came on foot. All were provided for.

The Mexican senoritas really had a refining influence on the frontier population. Many of them had been educated at convents, and all of them were good Catholics. They called the American men "Los God-dammes," and the American women "Las Camisas-Colorados." If there is anything that a Mexican woman despises it is a red petticoat. They are exceedingly dainty in their underclothing,--wear the finest linen they can afford; and spend half their lives over the washing machine. The men of northern Mexico are far inferior to the women in every respect.

This accretion of female population added very much to the charms of frontier society. The Mexican women were not by any means useless appendages in camp. They could keep house, cook some dainty dishes, wash clothes, sew, dance, and sing,--moreover, they were expert at cards, and divested many a miner of his week's wages over a game of monte.

As Alcalde of Tubac under the government of New Mexico, I was legally authorized to celebrate the rites of matrimony, baptize children, grant divorces, execute criminals, declare war, and perform all the functions of the ancient El Cadi.

The records of this primitive period are on file in the Recorder's office of the Pueblo of Tucson, Pima County.

Tubac became a kind of Gretna Green for runaway couples from Sonora; as the priest there charged them twenty-five dollars, and the Alcalde of Tubac tied the knot gratis, and gave them a treat besides.

I had been marrying people and baptizing children at Tubac for a year or two, and had a good many godchildren named Carlos or Carlotta according to gender, and began to feel quite patriarchal, when Bishop Lame sent down Father Mashboef, (Vicar Apostolic,) of New Mexico, to look after the spiritual condition of the Arizona people.

It required all the sheets and tablecloths of the establishment to fix up a confessional room, and we had to wait till noon for the blessing at breakfast; but worse than all that, my commadres, who used to embrace me with such affection, went away with their reybosas over their heads without even a friendly salutation.

It was "muy triste" in Tubac, and I began to feel the effects of the ban of the Church; when one day after breakfast Father Mashboef took me by the arm, (a man always takes you by the arm when he has anything unpleasant to say,) and said:--

"My young friend, I appreciate all you have been trying to do for these people; but these marriages you have celebrated are not good in the eyes of God."

I knew there would be a riot on the Santa Cruz if this ban could not be lifted. The women were sulky, and the men commenced cursing and swearing, and said they thought they were entitled to all the rights of matrimony.

My strong defense was that I had not charged any of them anything, and had given them a marriage certificate with a seal on it, made out of a Mexican dollar; and had given a treat and fired off the anvil. Still, although the Pope of Rome was beyond the jurisdiction of even the Alcalde of Tubac, I could not see the way open for a restoration of happiness.

At last I arranged with Father Mashboef to give the sanction of the Church to the marriages and legitimize the little Carloses and Carlottas with holy water, and it cost the company about $700 to rectify the matrimonial situation in Santa Cruz.

An idea that it was lonesome at Tubac would be incorrect. One can never be lonesome who is useful, and its was considered at the time that the opening of mines which yielded nothing before, the cultivation of land which lay fallow, the employment of labor which was idle, and the development of a new country were meritorious undertakings.

The table at Tubac was generously supplied with the best the market afforded, besides venison, antelope, turkeys, bear, quail, wild ducks, and other game, and we obtained through Guaymas a reasonable supply of French wines for Sunday dinners and the celebration of feast days.

It is astonishing how rapidly the development of mines increases commerce. We had scarcely commenced to make silver bars--"current with the merchant"--when the plaza at Tubac presented a picturesque scene of primitive commerce. Pack trains arrived from Mexico, loaded with all kinds of provisions. The rule was to purchase everything they brought, whether we wanted it or not. They were quite willing to take in exchange silver bars or American merchandise. Sometimes they preferred American merchandise. Whether they paid duties in Mexico was none of our business. We were essentially free traders.

The winter was mild and charming, very little snow, and only frost enough to purify the atmosphere. It would be difficult to find in any country of the world, so near the sea, such prolific valleys fenced in by mountains teeming with minerals. The natural elements of prosperity seem concentrated in profusion seldom found. In our primitive simplicity we reasoned that if we could take ores from the mountains and reduce them to gold and silver with which to pay for labor and purchase the productions of the valleys, a community could be established in the country independent of foreign resources. The result will show the success or failure of this Utopian scheme.

The usual routine at Tubac, in addition to the regular business of distributing supplies to the mining camps, was chocolate or strong coffee the first thing in the morning, breakfast at sunrise, dinner at noon, and supper at sunset.

Sunday was the day of days at Tubac, as the superintendents came in from the mining camps to spend the day and take dinner, returning in the afternoon. One Sunday we had a fat wild turkey weighing about twenty-five pounds, and one of my engineers asked permission to assist in the *cocina*. It was done to a charm, and stuffed with pine nuts, which gave it a fine flavor.

As we had plenty of horses and saddles, a gallop to the old Mission of San Jose de Turnucacori, one league south on the Santa Cruz River, afforded exercise and diversion for the ladies, especially of a Sunday afternoon. The old mission was rapidly going to ruin, but the records showed that it formerly supported a population of 3,500 people, from cultivation of the rich lands in the valley, grazing cattle, and working the silver mines. The Santa Cruz valley had been and could apparently again be made an earthly paradise. Many fruit trees yet remained in the gardens of the old mission church, and the "Campo Santo" walls were in a perfect state of preservation.

The communal system of the Latin races was well adapted to this country of oases and detached valleys. Caesar knew nearly as much about the governing machine as the sachem of Tammany Hall, or a governor in Mexico. At least, he enriched himself. In countries requiring irrigation the communal system of distributing water has been found to produce the greatest good for the greatest number. The plan of a government granting water to corporations, to be sold as a monopoly, is an atrocity against nature; and no deserving people will for long submit to it. The question will soon come up whether the government has any more right to sell the water than the air.

In the spring of 1857, a garden containing about two acres was prepared at Tubac, and irrigated by a canal from the Santa Cruz River. By the industry of a German gardener with two Mexican assistants, we soon produced all vegetables, melons, etc., that we required, and many a weary traveler remembers, or ought to remember, the hospitalities of Tubac. We were never a week without some company, and sometimes had more than we required; but nobody was ever charged anything for entertainment, horse-shoeing, and fresh supplies for the road. Hospitality is a savage virtue, and disappears with civilization.

As the ores in the Santa Rita Mountains did not make a satisfactory yield, we turned our explorations to the west of the Santa Cruz River, and soon struck a vein of petanque (silver copper glance) that yielded from the grass roots seven thousand dollars a ton. This mine was named in honor of the president of the company, "Heintzelman," which in German mining lore is also the name of the genius who presides over mines.

The silver bullion over expenses, which were about fifty per cent, was shipped, via Guaymas, to San Francisco, where it brought from 125 to 132 cents per ounce for the Asiatic market.

Silver bars form rather an inconvenient currency, and necessity required some more convenient medium. We therefore adopted the Mexican system of "boletas." Engravings were made in New York, and paper money printed on pasteboard about two inches by three in small denominations, twelve and one half cents, twenty-five cents, fifty cents, one dollar, five dollars, ten dollars. Each boleta had a picture, by which the illiterate could ascertain its denomination, viz: twelve and a half cents, a pig; twenty-five cents, a calf; fifty cents, a rooster; one dollar, a horse; five dollars, a bull; ten dollars, a lion. With these "boletas" the hands were paid off every Saturday, and they were currency at the stores, and among the merchants of the country and in Mexico. When a run of silver was made, anyone holding tickets could have them redeemed in silver bars, or in exchange on San Francisco. This primitive system of greenbacks worked very well,--everybody holding boletas was interested in the success of the mines; and the whole community was dependent on the prosperity of the company. They were all redeemed. Mines form the bank of Nature, and industry puts the money in circulation, to the benefit of mankind.

In the autumn of 1857 a detachment from the regiment of First Dragoons arrived in the Santa Cruz Valley, for the purpose of establishing a military post, and for the protection of the infant settlements. The officers were Colonel Blake, Major Stein, and Captain Ewell. The first military post was established at Calaveras, and the arrival of the officers made quite an addition to the society on the Santa Cruz.

Incident to the arrival of the military on the Santa Cruz was a citizens' train of wagons laden with supplies,--twelve wagons of twelve mules each,--belonging to Santiago Hubbell, of New Mexico. While he was encamped at Tubac I inquired the price of freight, and learned it was fifteen cents a pound from Kansas City. I inquired what he would charge to take back a freight of ores, and he agreed to haul them from the Heintzelman mine to Kansas City and a steamboat for twelve and a half cents a pound, and I loaded his wagons with ores in rawhide bags,--a ton to the wagon. This was the first shipment of ores, and a pretty "long haul."

Upon the arrival of these ores in the States they were distributed to different cities for examination and assay, and gave the country its first reputation as a producer of minerals. The average yield in silver was not enormous, as the ores contained a great deal of copper, but the silver yield was about fifteen hundred dollars to the ton.

In December, 1856, I purchased for the company the estate of "La Aribac," or Arivaca, as it is called by Americans. This place is a beautiful valley encompassed by mountains, and containing only a few leagues of land. It was settled by Augustine Ortiz, a Spaniard, in 1802, and title obtained from the Spanish government. The ownership and occupation descended to his two sons, Tomas and Ignacio Ortiz, who obtained additional title from the Mexican Republic in 1833, and maintained continuous occupation until 1856, when they sold to the company for a valuable consideration.

The validity of the title has been denied by the United States, notwithstanding the obligations of the treaty, and is now pending before the United States Land Court, with the prospect of an appeal to the United States Supreme Court, with a fair prospect of the ultimate loss of the property. The company conveyed the property with all mines and claims in Arizona to the writer, on the 2nd January, 1870,--a woful heritage.

In the early months of 1857, everything was going well in the Santa Cruz valley. The mines were yielding silver bullion by the most primitive methods of reduction. The farmers were planting with every prospect of a good crop. Emigrants were coming into the country and taking up farms. Merchants were busy in search of the Almighty Dollar or its representative.

The only disturbing element in the vicinity was a little guerilla war, going on in Sonora between two factions for the control of the State government. Gaudara was the actual governor, and had been so for many years, during which time he had accumulated a handsome fortune in lands, mills, mines, merchandise, live stock, and fincas. He was a sedate and dignified man, much respected by the natives, and especially polite and hospitable to foreigners. Pesquiera was an educated savage, without property or position, and naturally coveted his neighbor's goods. Consequently a revolution was commenced to obtain control of the governorship of the State; and just the same as when King David sought refuge in the cave of Adullam, all who were in debt, all who were refugees, all who were thieves, and all who were distressed, joined Pesquiera to rob Guadara. This is all there was,--or ever is, to Mexican revolutions.

On the discovery of gold in California, many Mexicans went from Sonora to California and remained there. Among these was one Ainsa, of Manila descent, married to a native of Sonora, who migrated to California with a large family of girls and boys in 1850, and had a Bank and Mexican Agency on the northwest corner of Clay and Montgomery streets, where there was the usual sign,--

    SE COMPRA ORO   Up Stairs

The girls of the Ainsa family grew to womanhood, and carried the beauty and graces of Sonora to a good market. They all married Americans, and married well.

As Helen of Sparta caused the Trojan War, and many eminent women have caused many eminent wars, there was no reason why the Ainsa women should not take part in the little revolution going on in their native State (Sonora). Their husbands could then become eminent men, annex the State of Sonora to the United States, and become governors and senators. It was a laudable ambition on the part of the Ainsa women, and their husbands were eminently deserving,--in fact, their husbands were already the foremost men in California in political position. One of them had been a prominent candidate for the United States Senate, and the others had occupied high position in Federal and State service, and were highly respected among their fellow citizens. In this state of affairs the eldest brother,--Augustine, was despatched to Sonora to see what arrangements could be made with Pesquiera if the Americans would come from California and help him oust Gaudara.

Pesquiera was in desperate straits, and agreed to whatever was necessary; the substance of which was that the Americans should come with five hundred men, well armed, and assist him in ousting Guadara and establishing himself as governor of Sonora. After that the Americans could name whatever they wanted in money or political offices, even to the annexation of the State, which was at that time semi-independent of Mexico.

Augustine, the Envoy Extraordinary and Minister Plenipotentiary, returned to California with the agreement in writing; and the Americans immediately began to drum up for recruits; but the prosperity of California was so great that but a few could be persuaded to leave a certainty for an uncertainty. The Americans in California actually started for Sonora with less than fifty men, with vague promises of recruits by sea. The records of the ferryman on the Colorado River show that they crossed the river with only forty-two men and a boy.

With this meager force these infatuated and misguided men pushed one hundred and thirty-two miles across a barren desert to the boundary line of Mexico at the Sonoita (Clover Creek), where there is a little stream of water struggling for existence in the sands. At the Sonoita the invaders were met by a proclamation from Pesquiera, forwarded through Redondo, the Prefect of Altar, warning them not to enter the State of Sonora. When men have resolved on destruction, reason is useless, and they paid no attention to the order, and crossed the boundary line of Mexico with arms and in hostile array. When they reached the vicinity of Altar they diverged from the main road to the west, and took the road to Caborca.

The only possible reason for this movement is that they may have expected reinforcements by sea, as Caborca is the nearest settlement to a little port called Libertad, where small ships could land. Be this as it may, no reinforcements ever came: and this little handful of Americans soon found themselves hemmed in at the little town of Caborca without hope or succor. They were the very first gentlemen of the States, mostly of good families, good education, and good prospects in California. What inhuman demon ever induced them to place themselves in such position, God only knows. Many of them left their wives and families in California, and all of them had warm friends there.

Pesquiera issued a bloodthirsty proclamation, in the usual grandiloquent language of Spain, calling all patriotic Mexicans to arms, to exterminate the invaders and to preserve their homes. The roads fairly swarmed with Mexicans. Those who had no guns carried lances, those who had no horses went on foot. Caborca was soon surrounded by Mexicans, and the forty-two Americans and one little boy took refuge in the church on the east side of the plaza.

This proved only a temporary refuge. An Indian shot a lighted arrow into the church and set it on fire. The Americans stacked arms and surrendered. My God! had they lost their senses? These forty-two American gentlemen, who had left their wives, children, and friends in California a month or two before under a contract with Pesquiera were butchered like hogs in the streets of Caborca, and neither God nor man raised hand to stop the inhuman slaughter.

They had not come within two hundred miles of my place, and nobody could have turned them from their purpose if they had. Many of them were old friends and acquaintances in California, and their massacre cast a gloom over the country.

There was only one redeeming act that ever came to my knowledge, and I know it to be true. When Pesquiera's order to massacre the invaders were read,

Gabilonda, second in command, swore he would have nothing to do with it, and mounting his horse swung the little boy Evans behind him and galloped away to Altar. Gabilonda carried him to Guaymas, from where he was afterwards sent to California.

It has been stated that the corpses were left in the streets for the hogs to eat, but the cure of Caborca assured me that he had a trench dug and gave them Christian interment. I never saw nor conversed with any of the leaders, but a detachment came up the Gila River to Tucson and Tubac, enlisting recruits, but could only raise twenty-five or thirty men. The invasion was generally discouraged by the settlers on the Santa Cruz. When they passed by Sopori on their way to join the main body, I remember very well the advice of old Colonel Douglas, a veteran in Mexican revolutions. He said,--

"Boys, unless you can carry men enough to whip both sides, never cross the Mexican line."

I was at Arivaca when the Santa Cruz contingent returned, badly demoralized, wounded, naked, and starving. The place was converted into a hospital for their relief, with such accommodations as could be afforded. Pesquiera was well aware of the adage that "dead men tell no tales." Crabb was beheaded, and his head carried in triumph to Pesquiera, preserved in a keg of Mescal, with the savage barbarity of the days of Herod. The contracts which would have compromised Pesquiera with the Mexican government were destroyed by fire. So ended the Crabb Expedition, one of the most ill-fated and melancholy of any in the bloody annals of Mexico.

The result of this expedition, commonly called "Crabb's," was that the Mexican government laid an embargo upon all trade with this side of the line, and business of all kinds was paralyzed.

Under these circumstances I crossed the desert on mule-back to Los Angeles, with only one companion, and went to San Francisco to take a rest.

III
War-Time in Arizona

The invasion of Sonora in the summer of 1857 by filibusters from California, generally called the "Crabb Expedition," caused the pall of death to fall on the boundary line of Mexico. Forty-two Americans had been massacred at Caborca, and many Mexicans had been killed. The abrasion was so serious that Americans were not safe over the Mexican boundary, and Mexicans were in danger in the boundaries of the United States.

Gabilonda, who was the only Mexican officer who protested against the massacre, came very near being mobbed by Americans in Tucson, although he was perfectly innocent of any crime,--on the contrary, deserved credit for his humanity in rescuing the boy Evans. Gabilonda was subsequently tried by a Mexican court martial organized by Pesquiera, the Governor of Sonora, and acquitted. He lived to a green old age as Collector of Mexican customs on the boundary line, and died honored and respected.

When I returned from San Francisco to the mines, in the winter of 1857, the country was paralyzed; but by the talisman of silver bars the mines were put in operation again, and miners induced to come in from Mexico. Christmas week the usual festival was given at Arivaca, and all the neighbors within a hundred miles invited.

In 1858 the business of the Territory resumed its former prosperity, and the sad events of the "Crabb Expedition" were smoothed over as far as possible. The government had subsidized an overland mail service at nearly a million a year, called the Butterfield line, with daily mails from St. Louis to San Francisco, running through Arizona. The mail service of the West has done a great deal to build up the country; and population came flocking into the Territory with high hopes of its future prosperity.

General Heintzelman obtained a furlough, and came out to superintend the mines. Colonel Samuel Colt, of revolver fame, succeeded him as president of the company, as he had contributed about two hundred and fifty thousand dollars in money and arms to its resources, with the intention of enlisting as much capital as might be required from New England. Machinery was constructed on the Atlantic seaboard, and hauled overland from the Gulf of Mexico to the mines,--1350 miles.

The Apaches had not up to this time given any trouble; but on the contrary, passed within sight of our herds, going hundreds of miles into Mexico on their forays rather than break their treaty with the Americans. They could have easily carried off our stock by killing the few vaqueros kept with them on the range, but refrained from doing so from motives well understood on the frontiers. There is an unwritten law among ranchmen as old as the treaty between Abraham and Lot.

In 1857 a company of lumbermen from Maine, under a captain named Tarbox, established a camp in the Santa Rita Mountains to whipsaw lumber at one hundred and fifty dollars per thousand feet, and were doing well, as the company bought all they could saw. They built a house and corral on the south side of the Santa Cruz River, on the road from Tucson to Tubac, called the Canoa. This wayside inn formed a very convenient stopping place for travelers on the road. One day twenty-five or thirty Mexicans rode into Tubac, and said the Apaches had made a raid on their ranches, and were carrying off some hundred head of horses and mules over the Babaquivera plain, intending to cross the Santa Cruz River between the Canoa and Tucson. The Mexicans wanted us to join them in a cortada (cut off), and rescue the animals, offering to divide them with us for our assistance; but remembering our treaty with the Apaches, and how faithfully they had kept it, we declined. They went on to the Canoa, where the lumbermen were in camp, and made the same proposition, which they accepted, as they were new in the country and needed horses and mules. The lumbermen joined the Mexicans, and as they could easily discern the course of the Apaches by the clouds of dust, succeeded in forming an ambuscade and fired on the Apaches when they reached the river. The Apaches fled at the fire, leaving the stolen stock behind.

The Mexicans made a fair division, and the mule trade was lively with the lumbermen and the merchants in Tucson. With the proceeds of their adventure the lumbermen added many comforts and luxuries to their camp at the Canoa on the Santa Cruz, and travelers reveled in crystal and whisky.

About the next full moon after this event, we had been passing the usual quiet Sunday in Tubac, when a Mexican vaquero came galloping furiously into the plaza, crying out: "Apaches! Apaches! Apaches!" As soon as he had recovered sufficiently to talk, we learned that the Apaches had made an attack on Canoa, and killed all the settlers.

It was late in the day; the men had nearly all gone to the mines, and we could only muster about a dozen men and horses; so we did not start until early next morning, as the Mexican said there were "Muchos Apaches."

When we reached the Canoa, a little after sunrise, the place looked as if it had been struck by a hurricane. The doors and windows were smashed, and the house a smoking ruin. The former inmates were lying around dead, and three of them had been thrown into the well, head foremost. We buried seven men in a row, in front of the burnt houses.

As well as could be ascertained by the tracks, there must have been fully eighty Apaches on horseback. They carried off on this raid 280 head of animals from the Canoa and the adjoining ranches.

There were some companies of the First Dragoons eating beef at Fort Buchanan. The commanding officer was notified, and sent some troops in pursuit, but the Apaches were in their strongholds long before the dragoons saddled their horses.

The pursuit of Apaches is exceedingly dangerous, as they are very skillful in forming ambuscades, and never give a fair fight in an open field. Their horsemanship is far superior to American troops, who are for the most part foreigners, and exceedingly awkward.

The second serious trouble with the Apaches was brought about by a far more foolish cause than the first, and it was much more disastrous.

In the winter of 1857 a somber colored son of Erin came along on foot to the presidio of Tubac, and solicited the rights of hospitality, food and a fire. Whether he had been run out of California by the Vigilance Committee, as many of our "guests" had been, or was escaping legitimate justice, was not in question; the imperative cravings of the stomach admit of very scant ceremony; so I took John Ward in to dinner, and provided him with all the comforts of home.

At bed-time he asked me if he might sleep in the front room by the fire; to which I reluctantly consented, taking good care to lock and bar the door between us.

The next morning after breakfast I gave John Ward some grub, and advised him to push on to Fort Buchanan, on the Sonoita, where he could probably get some employment.

He went on to the Sonoita and took up a ranch, forming a temporary partnership with a Mexican woman, according to the customs of the country at that time.

She had a little boy who also appeared to be partly of Celtic descent, as he had a red head, and was nicknamed "Micky Free." This probably formed the only matrimonial tie between John Ward and the Mexican woman. In the course of time John Ward got a hay contract, a wagon, and a few yoke of oxen, and appeared to be thriving at Uncle Sam's expense. Fort Buchanan was garrisoned by a portion of the First Regiment of dragoons. The most of the men were Germans, and could not mount a horse without a step-ladder.

In the early part of 1858 John Ward got drunk, and beat his step-son Micky Free until he ran away to Sonora. Ward became so blind drunk that he could not find his oxen; so he went to the Fort and complained to Major Stein, the commanding officer, that the Apaches had stolen his oxen and carried off the woman's boy.

Major Stein was a very good man, and very capable of running a saw-mill in Missouri, where he came from. He listened to John Ward's tale of woe, and ordered out a detachment of the First Dragoons, under Lieutenant Bascomb, to pursue the Apaches and recover Micky Free and the oxen. Bascomb was a fine-looking young fellow, a Kentuckian, a West Pointer, and of course a gentleman; but he was unfortunately a fool; although his uncle, Preacher Bascomb, of Lexington, was accounted a very eminent clergyman of the Presbyterian Church. This is a very different family from Bascomb of the Confederate X roads.

Lieutenant Bascomb's command pursued some Apaches, who had been raiding in Sonora, into the Whetstone Mountains, where they called a parley. The Apaches were summoned to camp ***under a white flag***; and feeling perfectly innocent of having committed a crime against the Americans, fearlessly presented themselves before Lieutenant Bascomb and his boys in blue. They positively denied having seen the boy or stolen the oxen; and they told the truth, as was well known afterward; but the Lieutenant was not satisfied, and ordered them seized and executed.

Four Apache chiefs were seized and tied. Cochise (in the Apache dialect Wood) managed to get hold of a knife, which he had concealed, cut his bonds, and escape. He was a very brave leader, and after having wreaked a terrible vengeance for the treachery of American troops to the Apaches, died in peace at the Indian Agency in the Chiricahua Mountains, 1874.

The war thus inaugurated by this Apache chieftain lasted fourteen years, and has scarcely any parallel in the horrors of Indian warfare. The men, women, and children, killed; the property destroyed, and the detriment to the settlement of Arizona cannot be computed. The cost of the war against Cochise would have purchased John Ward a string of yokes of oxen reaching from the Atlantic to the Pacific; and as for his woman's son, Micky Free, he afterwards became an Indian scout and interpreter, and about as infamous a scoundrel as those who generally adorn that profession. I am on very friendly terms with him and all his family, and would not write a word in derogation of his character, or of his step-father, John Ward, but to vindicate history.

The Vigilance Committee of San Francisco sent a considerable number of unsavory immigrants to Arizona, who with the refugees from Mexico, Texas and Arkansas, rendered mule property rather insecure in the early days. Gambling has been an industrial pursuit since the first settlement of the country, and the saloon business flourishes with the prosperity of the times. Strange to say, amidst this heterogeneous population there has never been a vigilance committee.

The Company and the country (synonymous terms) continued to improve, with occasional interruptions by the Apaches, until the beginning of 1861, when the reverberations of the gun fired at Sumter were heard in the Arizona mountains. A newspaper had been started by the company at Tubac, called *The Arizonian*. Our mail came overland by Butterfield coaches, at the rate of a hundred miles a day, but at last we waited for "the mail that never came." In the spring of 1861 a coach was started out from the Rio Grande with thirteen of the bravest buckskin boys of the West, and ten or twelve thousand dollars in gold, to pay off the line and withdraw the service; but the Apaches waylaid the coach in Stein's Pass, killed all of the men, and captured the gold.

In the month of June the machinery was running smoothly at Arivaca, the mines were yielding handsomely, and two hundred and fifty employees were working for good wages, which were paid punctually every Saturday afternoon.

One day an orderly from Fort Buchanan rode up to headquarters and handed me a note from Lieutenant Chapin, enclosing a copy of an order from the commanding officer of the Military Department:--

Santa Fe, June, 1861, Commanding Officer, Fort Buchanan:--

On receipt of this you will abandon and destroy
your Post; burn your Commissary and Quartermasters'
stores, and everything between the Colorado

and Rio Grande that will feed an army.

  March out with your guns loaded, and do not permit any citizen within fifteen miles of your lines.

(Signed) Major General Lynde

A council of the principal employees was called, and the order laid before them. The wisest said we could not hold the country after the troops abandoned it,--that the Apaches would come down upon us by the hundred, and the Mexicans would cut our throats. It was concluded to reduce the ore we had mined, which was yielding about a thousand dollars a day, pay off the hands, and prepare for the worst.

About a week afterwards the Apaches came down by stealth, and carried off out of the corral one hundred and forty-six horses and mules.

The Apaches are very adroit in stealing stock, and no doubt inherit the skill of many generations in theft. The corrals are generally built of adobe, with a gate or bars at the entrance. It was a customary practice for the Apaches to saw an entrance through an adobe wall with their horsehair ropes (cabrestas).

The corral at Arivaca was constructed of adobes, with a layer of cactus poles (ocquitillo) lengthwise between each layer of adobes. The Apaches tried their rope saw, but the cactus parted the rope. The bars were up, and a log chain wound around each bar and locked to the post; but they removed the bars quietly by wrapping their scrapes around the chain, to prevent the noise alarming the watchman. The steam engine was running day and night, and the watchman had orders to go the rounds of the place every hour during the night; but the Apaches were so skillful and secretive in their movements that not the least intimation of their presence on the place was observed,--not even by the watchdogs, which generally have a keen scent for Indians.

At the break of day the Apaches gave a whoop, and disappeared with the entire herd before the astonished gaze of five watchmen, who were sleeping under a porch within thirty yards. A pursuit was organized as soon as possible; but the pursuers soon ran into an ambuscade prepared by the retreating Apaches, when three were killed and two wounded. The rest returned without recovering any of the stock.

This loss of stock made very lonesome times at Arivaca, as it could not be replaced in the country, and we had no animals to haul ores, fuel, or provisions; only a few riding and ambulance animals, which had to be kept in stables and fed on grain.

About the same time the Apaches made an attack on the Santa Rita Mining Hacienda, and the eastern side of the Santa Cruz River had to be abandoned.

At Tubac, the headquarters of the company, where the old Mexican cuartel furnished ample room for storage, about a hundred and fifty thousand dollars worth of merchandise, machinery and supplies were stored. The Apaches, to the number of nearly a hundred, surrounded the town and compelled its evacuation. The plunder and destruction of property was complete. We had scarcely a safe place to sleep, and nothing to sleep on but the ground.

The women and children were escorted to the old pueblo of Tucson, where the few people remaining in the Territory were concentrated; and they remained there in a miserable condition until the troops arrived from California under General James A. Carlton, United States Army, commonly called "Carlton's Column."

General Carlton, upon arriving in the Territory, issued an order declaring martial law between the Colorado and the Rio Grande. These troops garrisoned the country between the rivers, and drove out the rebel troops, who had come in from Texas under the Confederate government.

After the abandonment of the Territory by the United States troops armed Mexicans in considerable numbers crossed the boundary line, declaring that the American government was broken up, and they had come to take their country back again. Even the few Americans left in the country were not at peace among themselves,--the chances were that if you met in the road it was to draw arms, and declare whether you were for the North or the South.

The Mexicans at the mines assassinated all the white men there when they were asleep, looted the place, and fled across the boundary to Mexico. The smoke of burning wheat-fields could be seen up and down the Santa Cruz valley, where the troops were in retreat, destroying everything before and behind them. The government of the United States abandoned the first settlers of Arizona to the merciless Apaches. It was impossible to remain in the country and continue the business without animals for transportation, so there was nothing to be done but to pack our portable property on the few animals we kept in stables, and strike out across the deserts for California.

With only one companion, Professor Pumpelly, and a faithful negro and some friendly Indians for packers, we made the journey to Yuma by the fourth of July, where we first heard of the battle of Bull Run. Another journey took us across the Colorado Desert to Los Angeles, and thence we went by steamer to San Francisco, and thence via Panama to New York.

It was sad to leave the country that had cost so much money and blood in ruins, but it seemed to be inevitable. The plant of the Company at this time in machinery, materials, tools, provisions, animals, wagons, etc., amounted to considerably over a million dollars, but the greatest blow was the destruction of our hopes,--not so much of making money as of making a country. Of all the lonesome sounds that I remember (and it seems ludicrous now), most distinct is the crowing of cocks on the deserted ranches. The very chickens seemed to know that they were abandoned.

We were followed all the way to Yuma by a band of Mexican robbers, as it was supposed we carried a great amount of treasure, and the fatigue of the journey by day and standing guard all night was trying on the strongest constitution in the hot summer month of June.

An account of the breaking up of Arizona and our journey across the deserts to California has been given by Professor Pumpelly, in his book, "Across America and Asia." The subject is so repugnant that the harrowing scenes preceding the abandonment of the country are only briefly stated.

The Civil War was in full blast upon my arrival in New York, and the change of venue from Apache Land was not peaceful. The little balance to my credit from the silver mines was with William T. Coleman & Co., 88 Wall Street, and I put it up as margin on gold at $132 and sold for $250.

After resting a while in New York I went down to Washington, and found my old friend General Heintzelman in command of what was technically called "The Defenses of Washington." The capital of the nation was beleaguered!

The Civil War and its results set Arizona back about twenty years.

The location of the Iturbide Grant had been continued in Sonora and Lower California, under direction of Captain--afterwards General--Stone, an officer for the United States Army, of engineering ability. I had first become acquainted with him when he was quartermaster at Benicia Barracks, in California, and met him the last time when he was chief of staff to the Khedive of Egypt at Grand Cairo, on the Nile.

Pesquiera, the governor of Sonora, held the state in quasi-independence of Mexico, and drove the surveying party under Stone out of Mexico by force of arms.

The funds for the location and survey of the Iturbide Grant had been furnished by French bankers in San Francisco, and obtained by them through their correspondent in Paris. A large portion of the money had been contributed by the entourage of the Second Empire under Napoleon, as the French were desirous of getting a foothold in Mexico. The expulsion of Stone's locating and surveying party was considered an affront to France, as the survey and location were undertaken under a valid grant of land made by the Mexican government, and the French were not satisfied to lose the many millions of francs they had invested in the enterprise. The influence of the shareholders in the Iturbide land location finally caused the intervention of the French government.

It will be remembered that the first intervention was a joint occupation of Vera Cruz by French, English and Spanish; but the English and Spanish soon withdrew, and left the French to pull their own chestnut out of the fire.

The time was not ripe for the French intervention in Mexico until we were in the midst of the Civil War, when Napoleon seized the opportunity to set up Maximilian of Austria, as Emperor of Mexico, protected by French forces under Bazaine.

No doubt but Napoleon and the officials of the Second Empire sympathized with the government of the Confederate States, and would have given them substantial aid if they had dared; but the Russian Czar sent a fleet to New York as a warning,--and the French had had enough of Russians on their track.

It was expressly stipulated in France, upon the founding of the Maximilian Empire, that the obligations given for funds to carry on the survey and location of the Iturbide Grant should be inscribed and recognized as a public debt of the Empire, and such will be found a matter of record and history. Many Frenchmen, no doubt, keep them as companion souvenirs to the obligations of the Panama Canal. The Grant has never been located, and the Mexican government yet owes the heirs, in equity, the original million dollars.

The French, under Maximilian, occupied Mexico up to the American boundary line, and many Mexicans took refuge in the United States,--among them Pesquiera, the governor of Sonora. His camp was at the old Mission of Tumucacori, in the Santa Cruz Valley and his wife is buried there.

President Juarez, of Mexico, was a refugee at El Paso del Norte during the reign of Maximilian, in destitute circumstances, when I was enabled to furnish him with a hundred thousand dollars in gold on a concession of Lower California. The circumstances were recently related for the Examiner of San Francisco, by Senor Romero, the Mexican minister in Washington.

During the brief existence of the Maximilian Empire in Mexico, many Americans flocked to the capital for adventures, as sympathizers with the government of the Confederate States, and consequently with the occupation of Mexico.

The late Senator Gwin of California was the acknowledged leader of the Americans, and it was rumored that he was to be created Duke of Sonora, but I never believed that the sterling old Democrat would have accepted a title of nobility.

The battle of Gettysburg sealed the fate of the Maximilian Empire, as well as the fate of the empire of the United States. The Mexican Empire and the French Empire have both passed away like dreams, but the Empire of the People grows stronger every year.

IV
Arizona a Territory at Last

When the Civil War was nearly over, General Heintzelman accompanied me on a call at the executive mansion, to solicit the organization of a territorial government for Arizona.

President Lincoln listened to my tale of woe like a martyr, and finally said, "Well, you must see Ben Wade about that."

I subsequently called upon Senator Wade of Ohio, the chairman of the Committee on Territories, and repeated my story of Arizona.

The bluff old Senator said, "O, yes, I have heard of that country,--it is just like hell--all it lacks is water and good society."

He finally consented to attend a meeting at the President's, to discuss the subject.

Ashley of Ohio was chairman of the Committee on Territories in the House, and readily agreed to favor the organization of a territorial government. In a few days President Lincoln appointed an evening, to hear the Delegation in favor of Arizona from 8 to 12. The chairmen of the committees on Territories attended, and General Heintzelman and some other friends were present. I presented the maps, historical data, some specimens of minerals and Indian relics, and after a long conference and some interesting stories by the President, the organization of a territorial government for Arizona was agreed upon.

The country was at that time under martial law,--General Carlton. If any system of government is repellent to Americans it is martial law. Whatever may be the expense of juries, lawyers, witnesses, and courts, they form the only means civilized society has yet devised for the settlement of disputes. It is true that a territorial form of government was never contemplated by the framers of the Constitution, as no provision was made for such a form of government; but this omission is covered by the general welfare clause, which gives Congress the power to "provide for the general welfare."

The formula adopted in an Act of Congress organizing a Territory, is "An Act to provide a provisional government, etc., etc., etc." In course of time, no doubt, all the Territories will be admitted as States, as the territorial form of government is not provided for as a permanency by the Constitution, and is moreover anomalous in the American system. The people residing in the Territories are to a considerable extent disfranchised politically, and are not, in fact, full-fledged American citizens. The idea of taxation without representation is irritating to their sense of justice, and for many other cogent reasons Congress will be forced by public opinion to admit the Territories to all the rights of sovereign States.

The delegate from New Mexico and myself sat at a table, and drew up a bill dividing New Mexico into nearly equal parts by the hundred and eleventh degree of longitude west; and providing for the organization of "The Territory of Arizona" from the western half. The bill soon became an Act of Congress, and was approved by President Lincoln on the twenty-third of February, 1863.

The offices were divided out among the supporters of the measure at an oyster supper, and as I was apparently to get nothing but the shells, I fortified myself with a drink, and exclaimed, "Well, gentlemen, what is to become of me?"

They seemed not to have thought about that, and the Governor-elect said:

"O, we will give you charge of the Indians, you are acquainted with them."

So I was appointed "Superintendent of Indian Affairs." The salary of the office was two thousand dollars a year, payable in greenbacks worth about thirty-three cents on the dollar in the currency of Arizona.

Arrangements were made for the transportation of my new colleagues across the plains at government expense; but I took Ben Holladay's coach at Kansas City, and crossed the continent to Sacramento, and thence by river steamer to San Francisco. The Indian goods had been shipped to Yuma.

In San Francisco I met my old friend, J. Ross Browne, who had just returned from Europe, and invited him to accompany me through Arizona at my expense. He afterwards wrote an account of the journey, "Wanderings in the Apache Country," published by Harpers.

Archbishop Alemany, whom I had known as a parish priest in Kentucky, called upon me in San Francisco, and asked if I would take a couple of priests down to Arizona, to restore the service among the Indians at the old Mission of San Xavier del Bac on the Santa Cruz, to which I assented with great pleasure.

After a voyage by sea from San Francisco to Los Angeles, I presented my orders from the Secretary of War to the commanding officer at Drumm Barracks for an escort of cavalry and transportation to Arizona; and prepared for the journey across the Colorado Desert.

We arrived at Yuma just before Christmas, and during Christmas week regaled the Yumas, Cocopas, and neighboring tribes of Indians with their first presents from Uncle Sam. After distributing the Indian goods at Yuma, we proceeded upon the Gila River some two hundred miles to the Pima village, where my old friends, the Pima Indians, gave a warm welcome, not entirely on account of the Indian goods.

At the Pima villages one Sunday, I requested the priests to celebrate the mass, and tell the Indians something about God,--remembering my own failure in teaching theology. The troops were drawn up, the Indians assembled, and Father Bosco through my interpreter preached the first sermon the Pima Indians ever heard.

At dinner, the good Father took me by the ear, and said, "What for you make me preach to these savages?--they squat on the ground, and laugh at me like monkeys."

The next place for the distribution of Indian goods was at the Mission of San Xavier del Bac, three leagues south of Tucson, among the Papagos, a christianized branch of the great Pima tribe. The Papago chiefs were my old friends and acquaintances, and received the priests with fireworks and illuminations. They knew of our coming, and had swept the church and grounds clean, and ornamented the altar with mistletoe.

The Indians had been expecting the priests for many years,----

> For the Jesuits told them long ago
> As sure as the water continued to flow,
> The sun to shine, and the grass to grow,
> They would come again to the Papago.

I installed the priests in the old Mission buildings, and turned over the goods intended for the Papagos for distribution at their convenience.

I met an old friend at the Mission called "Buckskin Alick," who had lived there all through the war without reading a newspaper or changing his clothes. As nails were scarce, Buckskin Alick had constructed a mill held together by rawhides, and was grinding wheat for the Papagos. In the meantime he had taken up with a Papago girl, to the scandal of the tribe. The priests told him he must marry the girl or leave. He appealed to me for protection, but I told him I had resigned my sacerdotal functions to the priest. He married the girl, and kept the mill.

In 1863 a considerable number of prospectors had come into Arizona, mostly from the California side, on account of discoveries of gold on the Hassayamp. Old Pauline Weaver was the discoverer, as he had been a trapper and pioneer since 1836. His name is carved on the walls of the Casa Grande with that date.

The gold washers there were doing very well, and ranches began to be established on the river. But the Apaches were not inclined to leave the settlers in peace when they had some fine horses and mules, and some fat cattle. So the Tonto Apaches made a raid on the Hassayamp, and carried off nearly all the stock.

King Woolsey had come into the country then, and was a prominent man among the settlers, and undoubtedly a very brave one; so he raised a company to go after the Tontos. (As every one knows, "tonto" means "fool.")

There were not more than twenty-five men, including some friendly Maricopas. They were well armed, but their commissariat consisted principally of panole and jerkey.

They followed the Indians across the Verde to a place about half way between Globe and the Silver King, where they came to a parley. The tanks there are surrounded by rough ledges of basalt rocks, and the country in the vicinity is covered by scoriae, as though a volcano had vomited the refuse of the subterranean world to disfigure nature.

The Indians came in slowly for a talk, but were insolent and defiant. Delshay, the Tonto chief, demanded a blanket and some coffee and whisky. The Americans had neither coffee nor whisky for their own use, and he was quite put out about it, but partook of panole and jerked beef.

The parley was very unsatisfactory, as the Indians were surly, and made demands which it was impossible to grant. There were about twenty-five Indians at the council, and fifty or more on the surrounding ledges. As the Indians became more hostile the situation became more serious, and it was evident to the Americans that they were surrounded, and in imminent danger of massacre.

Woolsey was not only a brave but a very intelligent man, and he saw at once that either the Americans or the Indians were to be slaughtered, so he said: "Boys, we have got to die or get out of this. Each of you pick out your Indian, and I will shoot the chief for a signal."

The fusillade commenced, and all the Indians that could run stampeded. The only American killed was Lennon, a half brother of Ammi White, my Indian agent at the Pima villages.

Lennon had picked out his Indian and sent a bullet to his heart; but the Indian in the agonies of death made a lunge at Lennon with his spear and transfixed him. They both fell at the Bloody Tanks in the embrace of death.

The Americans rescued Lennon's body, and having strapped it over a pack mule, carried it away to the next camp, where it was buried with Christian services at the foot of an aspen tree.

The Americans brought away twenty-four scalps.

After the Bloody Tanks affair some of the men engaged in it came into the Pima villages, where I was in camp. J. Ross Browne, who was with me, took down the account in short hand, and I made a list of the Americans engaged in the expedition. I remember, when Browne got through with his stenography, he asked one of the men if he had any Indian relics. The man replied, "Yes, I have got some jerked years," and he presented Browne about a dozen "jerked years" strung on buckskin.

I concluded to make a scout up country and see what was going on among the Indians, and as there were no troops at my command I organized a company of Pimas and Maricopas as scouts. They had recently received arms and ammunition from the government, and I had uniforms and swords enough for the officers. They soon learned to drill, and already knew how to shoot.

The commissariat was not quite up to military regulations, but we set out all the same, following along the Hassayamp to Antelope Peak, when we turned east by Walnut Creek to the Verde over an infernal trail.

The way down the Verde was not much better, as the Black Canon has never been considered strewn with roses; but we hunted and fished to the junction of the Verde and Salt River without seeing any Apaches.

The only "sign" we saw was cut on a tree,--twenty-four Americans and twenty-four arrows pointed at them, which the Pimas interpreted to me as the number of Americans the Apaches threatened to kill in retaliation.

There was not a soul on the Verde, and not a white man nor a house on the Salt River, from the junction of the Verde to its confluence with the Gila. We camped at the "Hole-in-the-Rock," and next morning crossed Salt River at the peak about Tempe, and crossed over to the Pima villages, glad enough to get to that haven of rest. It was 100 miles to Tucson, and 280 miles to Yuma, and not a soul nor any provisions between the two places.

There was no great inducement to stay in the Territory at that time, except for people who had an insane ambition for orchestral fame on the golden harps of New Jerusalem. Many of the people had read about the government of the United States, in school books; and perhaps had enjoyed the felicity of hearing a Fourth of July oration in youth; but these were myths of antiquity in Arizona. There was no government of any consequence, and even what there was was conducted on the Democratic principle, not for protection but for revenue only.

I anticipated the fourteenth amendment, and distributed the Indian goods without regard to race, color or former condition of servitude. Anybody that came along in need of blankets or tobacco was freely supplied. I wound up the Indian service with loss of about $5,000 out of my own pocket.

At camp on the Hassayamp, Henry Wickenburg came in with some specimens of gold quartz he had found out to the west, at a place subsequently called Vulture, and wanted me to buy the find. I said, "Henry, I don't want to buy your mine, but I will give you twenty-five dollars' worth of grub and a meerschaum pipe if you will go away and leave me alone."

I was also importuned to purchase Miguel Peralta's title from the King of Spain for the Salt River Valley; but my experience with Spanish grants in Texas, California and Arizona, did not incline me to invest, even if the grant had been made by the Pope of Rome, and guaranteed by the Continental Congress.

The only members of the Woolsey Expedition remaining in Arizona that I know of are Peeples of Phoenix, Chase of Antelope, and Blair at Florence.

The government of the United States can never recompense the people of Arizona for the atrocities committed by the Apaches. It will never do to make the plea that a government so vain-glorious and boastful could not have conquered this tribe of savages, if the will to do so had existed. Now, after forty years of devastation, the government pays the Apaches one hundred and fifty thousand dollars a year in goods to maintain a quasi peace. The settlers are not at any time secure against an Apache outbreak, and there are at the present time some Apaches on the war-path, which the government acknowledges its impotency to capture. "A Century of Dishonor" was a well written book, and contains many unpleasant truths.

In the meantime, while I was delivering the Indian goods, my colleagues in the territorial government had crossed the plains, and established the capital at a remote place in the northern mountains, which they called "Prescott," in honor of the Mexican historian. Just as was supposed, they quarreled all the way across the plains about who should be the first delegate to Congress from a Territory they had never seen.

Upon my arrival at Prescott they were perfectly disgusted to learn that I had already been declared a candidate, and was likely to get the votes of the people. The political machine had not then been organized, and the people had some say in the elections.

The election was held in due time, and I was elected the first delegate to Congress from Arizona.

The "carpet baggers" worked the Territory for all it was worth, as is evidenced by the public debt, which is three times as great as any State or Territory in the Union, *per capita*. The Capital was moved from town to town, as a political factor in the election of delegates, but now rests at Phoenix, in the Salt River Valley, where it will permanently remain, as no other place in the Territory can ever rival Phoenix in the abundance of all that contributes to the comfort and happiness of life. The soil is fertile, the climate healthful, and with water storage in reservoirs a city will grow equal to any on the Nile.

At this time there was not an inhabitant on Salt River where Phoenix now stands, and the Salt River Valley was a desolate and abandoned waste. It had been occupied some thousands of years ago by a race who cultivated the land by irrigation, and built houses and cities which have gone to ruin. The most diligent search has developed but few evidences of the extent of their civilization. They had not advanced very far, as they left no relics of either iron, copper, or steel. The land in cultivation would have supported a population of from fifty to a hundred thousand souls.

It is an excusable ambition for a man, especially in the Western country, to desire the honor of representing his State or Territory in Congress.

It was necessary to cross the deserts to San Francisco, and thence via Panama to New York and Washington.

I had scarcely taken my seat, when a distinguished-looking gentleman (Roscoe Conkling) came up and introduced himself, saying in a very pompous way:

"I observe you have drawn a front seat,--and as I presume you do not wish to debate, I shall feel very much obliged if you will have the courtesy to exchange seats with me."

I replied, "With the greatest pleasure, sir," and took a back seat, more becoming to my station.

In a few days the chairman of the Committee on Mileage came around to my seat, and said, "Poston, how is this?--your mileage is $7,200, and mine is only $300."

I replied, "Frank, what is the price of whisky in your district?"

He said, "About two dollars and a half per gallon."

"Well," I said, "it is fifteen dollars a gallon in Arizona--that equalizes the mileage."

He certified the account, and never said another word.

The salary was $5,000 a year, which added to the mileage, made $12,200;--but it all went, and a great deal more, in entertainment and presents at Washington. It was esteemed an honor to represent the Territory for which so many sacrifices had been made, and such severe hardships endured, and money was not spared to bring it to public notice on every suitable occasion.

The members of Congress usually manifest courtesy to delegates, as they are considered in a political sense orphans of the Republic, not having any vote nor in any other way being recognized as equals. They were not obliged at that time to serve on committees, nor expected to answer the roll-call. It was an easy berth for an indolent man without ambition or avarice.

The Thirty-eighth Congress was considered a very able assembly. The Civil War had brought the most illustrious men of the nation to the surface, and their acquaintance leaves a pleasant memory. When I look over their photographs, now it is like shuffling an old pack of cards which have been played out,--they have nearly all gone to the Upper Chamber,--in this world or the next. Grow and Holman are the only ones in the House now. Thaddeus Stevens was the leader of the House, and treated me with the most distinguished consideration,--even to the compliment of dining at my house,--which was unprecedented in his long public career. The old sinner said the exception was made because my wife was a Baptist.

I made but one speech, and that was on the subject of Indian affairs. An appropriation of one hundred and fifty thousand dollars was obtained for the construction of irrigating canals, to enable the Indians of Arizona to become self-supporting. This was the first instance in which irrigation was brought to the notice of the government.

President Lincoln was always accessible amid his heavy cares. As my family lived in the neighborhood where the President had been reared, my little girl made him a satchel of corn shucks from the field where he had hoed corn barefooted in the briars, thinking he might appreciate a souvenir from his old home. One afternoon I escorted my daughter to the executive mansion to deliver my present. The

President received it graciously, and made many enquiries about the old neighbors.

The 38th Congress passed the fourteenth amendment to the Constitution, and as the delegates could not vote they were requested to sign a paper giving their adhesion. I signed for Arizona; but it was a bitter pill.

The End.

www.bookjungle.com *email: sales@bookjungle.com fax: 630-214-0564 mail: Book Jungle PO Box 2226 Champaign, IL 61825*

The Codes Of Hammurabi And Moses
W. W. Davies

QTY

The discovery of the Hammurabi Code is one of the greatest achievements of archaeology, and is of paramount interest, not only to the student of the Bible, but also to all those interested in ancient history...

Religion **ISBN:** *1-59462-338-4* **Pages:**132 *MSRP $12.95*

The Theory of Moral Sentiments
Adam Smith

QTY

This work from 1749. contains original theories of conscience amd moral judgment and it is the foundation for systemof morals.

Philosophy **ISBN:** *1-59462-777-0* **Pages:**536 *MSRP $19.95*

Jessica's First Prayer
Hesba Stretton

QTY

In a screened and secluded corner of one of the many railway-bridges which span the streets of London there could be seen a few years ago, from five o'clock every morning until half past eight, a tidily set-out coffee-stall, consisting of a trestle and board, upon which stood two large tin cans, with a small fire of charcoal burning under each so as to keep the coffee boiling during the early hours of the morning when the work-people were thronging into the city on their way to their daily toil...

Childrens **ISBN:** *1-59462-373-2* **Pages:**84 *MSRP $9.95*

My Life and Work
Henry Ford

QTY

Henry Ford revolutionized the world with his implementation of mass production for the Model T automobile. Gain valuable business insight into his life and work with his own auto-biography... "We have only started on our development of our country we have not as yet, with all our talk of wonderful progress, done more than scratch the surface. The progress has been wonderful enough but..."

Biographies/ **ISBN:** *1-59462-198-5* **Pages:**300 *MSRP $21.95*

www.bookjungle.com email: sales@bookjungle.com fax: 630-214-0564 mail: Book Jungle PO Box 2226 Champaign, IL 61825

The Art of Cross-Examination
Francis Wellman

QTY

I presume it is the experience of every author, after his first book is published upon an important subject, to be almost overwhelmed with a wealth of ideas and illustrations which could readily have been included in his book, and which to his own mind, at least, seem to make a second edition inevitable. Such certainly was the case with me; and when the first edition had reached its sixth impression in five months, I rejoiced to learn that it seemed to my publishers that the book had met with a sufficiently favorable reception to justify a second and considerably enlarged edition. ..

Reference　　ISBN: *1-59462-647-2*　　Pages:412　　MSRP *$19.95*

On the Duty of Civil Disobedience
Henry David Thoreau

QTY

Thoreau wrote his famous essay, On the Duty of Civil Disobedience, as a protest against an unjust but popular war and the immoral but popular institution of slave-owning. He did more than write—he declined to pay his taxes, and was hauled off to gaol in consequence. Who can say how much this refusal of his hastened the end of the war and of slavery ?

Law　　ISBN: *1-59462-747-9*　　Pages:48　　MSRP *$7.45*

Dream Psychology Psychoanalysis for Beginners
Sigmund Freud

QTY

Sigmund Freud, born Sigismund Schlomo Freud (May 6, 1856 - September 23, 1939), was a Jewish-Austrian neurologist and psychiatrist who co-founded the psychoanalytic school of psychology. Freud is best known for his theories of the unconscious mind, especially involving the mechanism of repression; his redefinition of sexual desire as mobile and directed towards a wide variety of objects; and his therapeutic techniques, especially his understanding of transference in the therapeutic relationship and the presumed value of dreams as sources of insight into unconscious desires.

Psychology　　ISBN: *1-59462-905-6*　　Pages:196　　MSRP *$15.45*

The Miracle of Right Thought
Orison Swett Marden

QTY

Believe with all of your heart that you will do what you were made to do. When the mind has once formed the habit of holding cheerful, happy, prosperous pictures, it will not be easy to form the opposite habit. It does not matter how improbable or how far away this realization may see, or how dark the prospects may be, if we visualize them as best we can, as vividly as possible, hold tenaciously to them and vigorously struggle to attain them, they will gradually become actualized, realized in the life. But a desire, a longing without endeavor, a yearning abandoned or held indifferently will vanish without realization.

Self Help　　ISBN: *1-59462-644-8*　　Pages:360　　MSRP *$25.45*

www.bookjungle.com email: sales@bookjungle.com fax: 630-214-0564 mail: Book Jungle PO Box 2226 Champaign, IL 61825

QTY

	Title	ISBN	Price
☐	**The Rosicrucian Cosmo-Conception Mystic Christianity** by *Max Heindel*	ISBN: 1-59462-188-8	$38.95
	The Rosicrucian Cosmo-conception is not dogmatic, neither does it appeal to any other authority than the reason of the student. It is: not controversial, but is: sent forth in the, hope that it may help to clear...		New Age/Religion Pages 646
☐	**Abandonment To Divine Providence** by *Jean-Pierre de Caussade*	ISBN: 1-59462-228-0	$25.95
	"The Rev. Jean Pierre de Caussade was one of the most remarkable spiritual writers of the Society of Jesus in France in the 18th Century. His death took place at Toulouse in 1751. His works have gone through many editions and have been republished...		Inspirational/Religion Pages 400
☐	**Mental Chemistry** by *Charles Haanel*	ISBN: 1-59462-192-6	$23.95
	Mental Chemistry allows the change of material conditions by combining and appropriately utilizing the power of the mind. Much like applied chemistry creates something new and unique out of careful combinations of chemicals the mastery of mental chemistry...		New Age Pages 354
☐	**The Letters of Robert Browning and Elizabeth Barret Barrett 1845-1846 vol II** by *Robert Browning* and *Elizabeth Barrett*	ISBN: 1-59462-193-4	$35.95
			Biographies Pages 596
☐	**Gleanings In Genesis (volume I)** by *Arthur W. Pink*	ISBN: 1-59462-130-6	$27.45
	Appropriately has Genesis been termed "the seed plot of the Bible" for in it we have, in germ form, almost all of the great doctrines which are afterwards fully developed in the books of Scripture which follow...		Religion/Inspirational Pages 420
☐	**The Master Key** by *L. W. de Laurence*	ISBN: 1-59462-001-6	$30.95
	In no branch of human knowledge has there been a more lively increase of the spirit of research during the past few years than in the study of Psychology, Concentration and Mental Discipline. The requests for authentic lessons in Thought Control, Mental Discipline and...		New Age/Business Pages 422
☐	**The Lesser Key Of Solomon Goetia** by *L. W. de Laurence*	ISBN: 1-59462-092-X	$9.95
	This translation of the first book of the "Lernegton" which is now for the first time made accessible to students of Talismanic Magic was done, after careful collation and edition, from numerous Ancient Manuscripts in Hebrew, Latin, and French...		New Age/Occult Pages 92
☐	**Rubaiyat Of Omar Khayyam** by *Edward Fitzgerald*	ISBN: 1-59462-332-5	$13.95
	Edward Fitzgerald, whom the world has already learned, in spite of his own efforts to remain within the shadow of anonymity, to look upon as one of the rarest poets of the century, was born at Bredfield, in Suffolk, on the 31st of March, 1809. He was the third son of John Purcell...		Music Pages 172
☐	**Ancient Law** by *Henry Maine*	ISBN: 1-59462-128-4	$29.95
	The chief object of the following pages is to indicate some of the earliest ideas of mankind, as they are reflected in Ancient Law, and to point out the relation of those ideas to modern thought.		Religion/History Pages 452
☐	**Far-Away Stories** by *William J. Locke*	ISBN: 1-59462-129-2	$19.45
	"Good wine needs no bush, but a collection of mixed vintages does. And this book is just such a collection. Some of the stories I do not want to remain buried for ever in the museum files of dead magazine-numbers an author's not unpardonable vanity..."		Fiction Pages 272
☐	**Life of David Crockett** by *David Crockett*	ISBN: 1-59462-250-7	$27.45
	"Colonel David Crockett was one of the most remarkable men of the times in which he lived. Born in humble life, but gifted with a strong will, an indomitable courage, and unremitting perseverance...		Biographies/New Age Pages 424
☐	**Lip-Reading** by *Edward Nitchie*	ISBN: 1-59462-206-X	$25.95
	Edward B. Nitchie, founder of the New York School for the Hard of Hearing, now the Nitchie School of Lip-Reading, Inc, wrote "LIP-READING Principles and Practice". The development and perfecting of this meritorious work on lip-reading was an undertaking...		How-to Pages 400
☐	**A Handbook of Suggestive Therapeutics, Applied Hypnotism, Psychic Science** by *Henry Munro*	ISBN: 1-59462-214-0	$24.95
			Health/New Age/Health/Self-help Pages 376
☐	**A Doll's House: and Two Other Plays** by *Henrik Ibsen*	ISBN: 1-59462-112-8	$19.95
	Henrik Ibsen created this classic when in revolutionary 1848 Rome. Introducing some striking concepts in playwriting for the realist genre, this play has been studied the world over.		Fiction/Classics/Plays 308
☐	**The Light of Asia** by *sir Edwin Arnold*	ISBN: 1-59462-204-3	$13.95
	In this poetic masterpiece, Edwin Arnold describes the life and teachings of Buddha. The man who was to become known as Buddha to the world was born as Prince Gautama of India but he rejected the worldly riches and abandoned the reigns of power when...		Religion/History/Biographies Pages 170
☐	**The Complete Works of Guy de Maupassant** by *Guy de Maupassant*	ISBN: 1-59462-157-8	$16.95
	"For days and days, nights and nights, I had dreamed of that first kiss which was to consecrate our engagement, and I knew not on what spot I should put my lips..."		Fiction/Classics Pages 240
☐	**The Art of Cross-Examination** by *Francis L. Wellman*	ISBN: 1-59462-309-0	$26.95
	Written by a renowned trial lawyer, Wellman imparts his experience and uses case studies to explain how to use psychology to extract desired information through questioning.		How-to/Science/Reference Pages 408
☐	**Answered or Unanswered?** by *Louisa Vaughan*	ISBN: 1-59462-248-5	$10.95
	Miracles of Faith in China		Religion Pages 112
☐	**The Edinburgh Lectures on Mental Science (1909)** by *Thomas*	ISBN: 1-59462-008-3	$11.95
	This book contains the substance of a course of lectures recently given by the writer in the Queen Street Hall, Edinburgh. Its purpose is to indicate the Natural Principles governing the relation between Mental Action and Material Conditions...		New Age/Psychology Pages 148
☐	**Ayesha** by *H. Rider Haggard*	ISBN: 1-59462-301-5	$24.95
	Verily and indeed it is the unexpected that happens! Probably if there was one person upon the earth from whom the Editor of this, and of a certain previous history, did not expect to hear again...		Classics Pages 380
☐	**Ayala's Angel** by *Anthony Trollope*	ISBN: 1-59462-352-X	$29.95
	The two girls were both pretty, but Lucy who was twenty-one who supposed to be simple and comparatively unattractive, whereas Ayala was credited, as her Bombwhat romantic name might show, with poetic charm and a taste for romance. Ayala when her father died was nineteen...		Fiction Pages 484
☐	**The American Commonwealth** by *James Bryce*	ISBN: 1-59462-286-8	$34.45
	An interpretation of American democratic political theory. It examines political mechanics and society from the perspective of Scotsman James Bryce		Politics Pages 572
☐	**Stories of the Pilgrims** by *Margaret P. Pumphrey*	ISBN: 1-59462-116-1	$17.95
	This book explores pilgrims religious oppression in England as well as their escape to Holland and eventual crossing to America on the Mayflower, and their early days in New England...		History Pages 268

www.bookjungle.com email: sales@bookjungle.com fax: 630-214-0564 mail: Book Jungle PO Box 2226 Champaign, IL 61825

Title	ISBN	Price	QTY
The Fasting Cure by *Sinclair Upton* — In the Cosmopolitan Magazine for May, 1910, and in the Contemporary Review (London) for April, 1910, I published an article dealing with my experiences in fasting. I have written a great many magazine articles, but never one which attracted so much attention... *New Age/Self Help/Health Pages 164*	*1-59462-222-1*	**$13.95**	☐
Hebrew Astrology by *Sepharial* — In these days of advanced thinking it is a matter of common observation that we have left many of the old landmarks behind and that we are now pressing forward to greater heights and to a wider horizon than that which represented the mind-content of our progenitors... *Astrology Pages 144*	*1-59462-308-2*	**$13.45**	☐
Thought Vibration or The Law of Attraction in the Thought World by *William Walker Atkinson* — *Psychology/Religion Pages 144*	*1-59462-127-6*	**$12.95**	☐
Optimism by *Helen Keller* — Helen Keller was blind, deaf, and mute since 19 months old, yet famously learned how to overcome these handicaps, communicate with the world, and spread her lectures promoting optimism. An inspiring read for everyone... *Biographies/Inspirational Pages 84*	*1-59462-108-X*	**$15.95**	☐
Sara Crewe by *Frances Burnett* — In the first place, Miss Minchin lived in London. Her home was a large, dull, tall one, in a large, dull square, where all the houses were alike, and all the sparrows were alike, and where all the door-knockers made the same heavy sound... *Childrens/Classic Pages 88*	*1-59462-360-0*	**$9.45**	☐
The Autobiography of Benjamin Franklin by *Benjamin Franklin* — The Autobiography of Benjamin Franklin has probably been more extensively read than any other American historical work, and no other book of its kind has had such ups and downs of fortune. Franklin lived for many years in England, where he was agent... *Biographies/History Pages 332*	*1-59462-135-7*	**$24.95**	☐

Name	
Email	
Telephone	
Address	
City, State ZIP	

☐ Credit Card   ☐ Check / Money Order

Credit Card Number	
Expiration Date	
Signature	

Please Mail to: Book Jungle
PO Box 2226
Champaign, IL 61825
or Fax to: 630-214-0564

ORDERING INFORMATION

web: *www.bookjungle.com*
email: *sales@bookjungle.com*
fax: *630-214-0564*
mail: *Book Jungle PO Box 2226 Champaign, IL 61825*
or PayPal *to sales@bookjungle.com*

Please contact us for bulk discounts

DIRECT-ORDER TERMS

**20% Discount if You Order
Two or More Books**
Free Domestic Shipping!
Accepted: Master Card, Visa,
Discover, American Express

www.ingramcontent.com/pod-product-compliance
Lightning Source LLC
Chambersburg PA
CBHW081329040426
42453CB00013B/2352